Tristia

Tristia

Carmen Bugan

Shearsman Books

First published in the United Kingdom in 2025 by
Shearsman Books Ltd
PO Box 4239
Swindon
SN3 9FN

Shearsman Books Ltd Registered Office
30–31 St. James Place, Mangotsfield, Bristol BS16 9JB
(this address not for correspondence)

www.shearsman.com

ISBN 978-1-84861-966-1

ACKNOWLEDGEMENTS
Some of these poems have been published in *Literary Matters, Oxford
Magazine, Hypertext, Residential College Magazine, Shearsman magazine,
Floreat Domus, Monk,* and *The Irish Times.* The Oxford Centre for Life Writing,
the Poetry School in London, Gotham Writers' Workshop, the Geneva Writers'
Group, the International Women Writers Guild, and more recently
New York University in Abu Dhabi, helped me believe in my writing and
teaching enough to get through very challenging moments: I am honored and
grateful. Christopher Ricks, Carl Schmidt, Pramila Venkateswaran, Carolyn
Emerson, Raji Sunder-Rajan, Eilean Ni Chuilleanain, Gerard Smyth, Jane
Griffiths, Duncan Wu, Lucy Newlyn, Elleke Boehmer, and Philip Fried have
continued to support me and my work during an extremely difficult time
in my life: thank you. My family has given me courage to keep going. My
children, Alisa and Stefano, are the substance and the form in these poems.
I thank Andrew Locking https://www.andrewswalks.co.uk/ for the kind
permission to use his photograph for the cover. Finally, I would like to express
my profound gratitude to my editor and publisher, Tony Frazer, for doing the
extraordinary thing almost no one does these days, which is to demonstrate
steadfast loyalty to his authors over time.

CONTENTS

To my father, in memoriam

Leaving

We will leave behind those we love,
Saddened by how little time
We were granted with them.

Those who caused us pain
Will be left holding the chains
They have fashioned for us.

We are rising on the back of the wind.
Soon we will leap through rainbows
Where our souls will let go of grief.

Night in the Church

In memory of Tanti *Bălașa*

The congregation chose to have your wake in church.
They placed your coffin on a table overfilled with flowers,
Your frame, smaller on white satin – coffin like a crib –
Makes me think again about the time before birth,
When the body is womb-housed,
Outside memory, inside mysterious life.

Icon under your crossed hands, cross, candle:
As it's always been, in custom and in ceremony.
Yet, unlike others, in your last day above the ground
You are lying in the center of the church.
What did you say all night to the altar saints?
And what were your instructions on the way to Heaven?
I think of you being honored as a stateswoman.

And stately you were in the communist factory
Kitchen, commandeering a small team of cooks:
Workers lining up for the bowl of sour soup
Worshipped you as much as their mothers: to my taste,
No one has surpassed your cooking skills.
No one has measured ingredients more precisely,
Immeasurable in kindness to everyone you were.

You loved red wine and loved singing hymns,
You were the choir mistress. Last we met
You offered the plum wine. Together with
The big family, we sang. And laughed.
We gossiped in those flowery native words.

I remember you wanted me for your daughter,
How I never left my mother, and how she
Would have never let me go, despite the hardship

And the pain of those last few years in Romania.
So, you kept asking me to postpone the bus home,
Wait for the next, and the next, till the last one was due.

"Come once more before you leave this time,"
You asked. Today I can't remember if I did.
Today your sister (my mother) is crying
On the phone and sending pictures of you in the coffin,
Your face out of focus, a table with bread and fruit,
A stand with candles that become smaller, kneeling
In the sand. You come to me in that soft light
Around your table when Dad cried as we sang.

September 18, 2021

So

You say, "now we shall begin to dance,"
You have thought about your moves –
Your share of guilt, your steps on ice
(For you are saying that we're skating
Figures who entered the performance) –
But that you can't control the steps
I, who am "not a partner," will choose.

But dancing, just like marriage, requires
Agreeing on rules, the backward and forward
Steps, followed by graceful body moves,
Breathing together the same air, sharing
Space, so that the vision of performance
Embodies harmonies of good intentions,
As two people unite to make their art.

So, if our marriage into a dance must turn –
Skate-dancing on the ice rink, in the glare
Of artificial lights, before spectators
(Who might be absent-minded, mind
You; or eager to laugh at us, or accuse)
Consider this: not even on solid ground
Can you waltz footloose.

Dancing, like marriage, is a practicing art
Into which we enter at our will.
Distill the moments we still have, my love,
And don't confuse dancing alone
(Which also asks for practiced skill)
With waltzing in pairs, where partners
Lead and follow each other by old rules.

November 2021

La Cinquantaine – Gabriel Marie
for Stefano

You say the cello has a human voice
That speaks to you these late afternoons
And nights of family tumult

When the strings of the four of us
Are plucked again and again,
Turned against their own music,
into wires.

Your sadness turns the melody
Into a story about you. I listen
To each nervous repetition:

The tremulous notes, the liquid
Trill of inner crying – through your fingers
Into the echoing wood.

Play it, play the instrument, and tell
It all, until, like me, you are told out
Sounded out, sounded through, and

Ready for the golden notes of peace
Gathering upon the strings: search
For that one and only melody.

I hear you, my son, and feel with you each
Loosened string, each one of us
Leaving this song to start a life anew.

13 December 2021

The Master's Field

For Alan Kingsley, in memoriam

When our friend sent news about you
Walking that final stretch of road, he asked
If I would write, because he thought it best
"To be reminded of friends and happy times."

Memories of the three of us playing like
Children at recess in the Master's Field
Between lectures on poetry, philosophy,
"Structural design with glass,"

Walks at Christ Church Meadows,
Strolls through St Catherine's Fields
And Magdalen's Deer Park, wine
And mussels, chess and hearty laughter—

Flooded me with such force
That I felt at a loss to find
Comforting words to offer
During your final days.

I remembered Mark's wedding
In Adelaide, the vineyard, the two of us
Walking in Sydney's Botanic Gardens,
With youth on our side.

Exchanging news with you became
A heartbreaking game of wait and see.
No one learns how to die young. Now
That you have gone, we are gathering

To celebrate the "one of us." You
Brimming with smiles, always calm,
Always thinking, then back to that inner smile
That kept us companionship in happy times.

*

Alan, you will hold the rest of us together
As much as memory does: gently and forever.
The picture of yourself you sent to me
Is of a boy playing on the floor with his father:

It's one I've never seen. It's a part of you
I never met before, my dear friend—a parting gift?
The little boy's eye light takes me by surprise
Like a wish half-fulfilled, or like a thought

That barely touches the mind, and leaves before
You have the chance to learn what it is. Tonight's
Salmon sky glowed in the garden, and, like your life,
Vanished before I could record it in my mind's eye.

I see Mark and you in the Master's Field at Balliol
In that moment before the Professor of Poetry's Lecture,
When it was so hard to tear myself from our chasing game,
To go learn about the fields of just and perfect words.

14 December 2021

Winter Solstice

Last night's moon
In the clear skies
Was big as a head on fire;

This frozen morning,
Its pallid face
Hangs above the street.

We are becoming still –
Trees under snow –
Winds tear our weakest parts.

We'll survive the season
Drawing strength
From inner depths.

*

Our longest night arrived,
In this comfortless season
When the road cracks underfoot.

The shortest day calls in the winter:
The unfeeling hearts in our family
Will tilt towards sunlight, hopefully.

Stony Brook, December 21, 2021

Interpretations

The story skirts around the words
But it can't be missed at the Saturday dusting
(Of the bookshelves, the mantelpiece),
No matter what's said about house cleaning.

Every weekend for a year and more
Our wedding photos and the neat stacks
Of books I set out for teaching
Suffer the passing of your dusting storm:

My photo at the garden party is felled
Face down, or moved facing the wall,
The two of us in Scotland on the beach,
Barefoot in sand after lovemaking:
Knocked to the floor.

As I Walked Out One Morning
Hangs half off the shelf.
Plato's *Ion* is sideways on the desk,
Anthologies thrown in a pile.
Why, why take your rage
On our pictures and my books?

Meanwhile, most of your
Underclothes and socks have vanished
From your dresser, the stack of sweaters too,
Pajamas, shirts, and God-knows-what.

They left an eerie space in their places.

This comes as you declare I am your wife;
We need to think together of the future.
I read the signs you leave each week
Around the emptying house,
In upturned spines of books:
I read, I think, I cry.

January 8, 2022

The Word

The word felled the children like an axe,

their heads bowed on the kitchen table

with all their golden curls, as if in prayer;

do not kiss them after saying that word.

January 18, 2022

January 25, 2022

A family watches the sunset
At West Meadow Beach,
Drinking hot chocolate
The father pours from a thermos.

The mother's camera is trained on the sky
Where the sun is doing its thing
That brings joy even to my betrayed heart.

The parents prepare for a selfie:
The woman takes the hat off her husband's head
And smooths his hair, which makes him kiss her,
And that makes the children laugh.

I turn back to the car, and there,
Reflected on the windshield,
I see them all, embracing,
Embraced by the glowing evening.

On the Eve

First, the shadow of her wings
Crisscrossed the shadow of the branches,
The change of light called me to the window
To see it flit twice across the grass.

She landed between the yew and maple
And folded her blue-grey wings.
Her long beak, yellow eyes,
Her twig-like legs perfectly poised,
One folded up, claws moving,
Her feathers artfully arranged –
She was a wild ballerina.

We were too far apart to know
If she was looking at me.
She came to stay. I wondered if
She was a spirit on an errand,
Because she stood for nearly an hour,
While in the house we oohed as we looked.
Even the hardened heart stirred
Witnessing such patient stillness.

The birds stopped their songs,
The squirrels froze mid-motion
And she became a grey heron statue
Next to the stone bird bath.

*

When I stepped outside,
She took two steps backwards,
Unstartled, making space.
She did not leave. I wanted her

To see me, say something to me:
She, who came from the wild
To land upon the struggling soul.

I read her composure:
"Stay still. Be patient. Concentrate."
I was eager to see her
Unfold her blue-tipped wings,
Take the gulp of air,
Climb out of the backyard,
Surveil our loveless house,
Embrace the hunting freedom,
As I wanted to leave but couldn't.

When the blue heron left
I felt like a loose feather that fell
From her faultlessly designed,
Purpose-loving wings.

Stony Brook, February 6, 2022

We're Not Going to Cross to the Other Side

"Those days in the garden with *Bunicu*," you say,
"When I would walk out of the house to find him
Sit on the chair in the sun, or binding tomatoes,
I felt like I was in the presence of someone very old
And at the same time young. *Bunicu* has something
Timeless about him, and I did not want those days to end.
Bunica in the kitchen, thinking and making only comfort.
There is where I felt at home, that was love.
I told you I never wanted to come back here."

I know, my son, but when we crossed the Sound back
My heart still hoped that we will find our home
Inside the home that sent us out;
Today a woman came to price it for the market.
The fight in the kitchen after. I never felt so angry.
"I feel weakening each day," you say,
"Finish this, take us out of here, please.
I'm losing trust in you the way
You go back and forth. Just end it, it's unbearable."
The woman said, "Why sell the house? It's a good dwelling.
You've everything you need in here."

*

I swear by your tears, your sister's, and mine,
I will end this. No child of mine will suffer
This misery again. No child of mine
Will be blue from crying for the want of peace.

February 12, 2022

A Prayer for Europe

The warring language floats in the winter air
At the words of one dictator. People forget
Preparations for Clean Monday to begin the war.

Across the border, children wake up
In the night, to the sound of bombs,
A neighborhood grocery store will turn to ruin,

And old men, together with young women
Will take up their guns, to join the army.
Old mistrust rises poisoning words.

If I could halt the madness with a call
To prayer, a reminder of old kindnesses
We all so easily tend to forget.

*

Today Europe is a woman
Whose body has been sliced by the birthing
Knife, over and over, her caesarean

Wound badly patched birth after birth,
Her womb crisscrossed; flesh hardened
Along ridges of history written in blood.

Protect its lifegiving womb, slice her no more.
Consider the early patches of snowdrops
Under the wheels of the tanks.

Would those who fly the bomber planes
Notice the change of seasons in the sky
For the peace it could bring, and fly back home?

Will neighborly kindness revisit memory?
The world lifts its hands in prayer as
Europe suffers.

Stony Brook, 27 February 2022

The Woodpecker in the Spring

Many things were written in the day, even
Before the sunrise: clouds, morning wind,
The lawyer's exorbitant bill, long-term despair,
Looping telephone call to Mother, the war.

But not the woodpecker's rapid tick-tock
In the waking maples beside
The left window of our bedroom
That I turned into a study-room last year.

It's true, today is not a freshly turned
Open page, the future is not an airy space
To fill entirely with lofty dreams.
But that call to the ancient renewal, is!

3 March, 2022

Wedding Ring

It's now loose
Again, like it was
At the beginning
Of our marriage

When I feared
It might slip
While swimming
In Lake Michigan.

The weight
From the children's births
Is finally gone, the body
Recalls its youthful shape;
Only the skin's weariness,
Betrays the passing of time.

What will I do with this ring
Once it is all over,
The house sold
The children's faith
In *familia / famiglia*
Quartered and bartered?

I shall bury it under a tree
At West Meadow,
Where I talk to the sea
About beginning and endings,
And where – once gone –
I shall never return.

March 22, 2022

End of March

Sea in perfect stillness: the art
Of conversation with the sky.
Clouds seem to drift to shore
Over pebbles, gold iridescent shells.

The green algae on the promontory
Look like new moss bright in sunlight.

Geese draw waves in the rain-promising sky
Flying in large obstreperous flocks.

On the streets, on the drive back home,
The first patches of purple-pink rhododendrons –
By kitchen windows or front porches –
Suddenly purple-pink, spring-lit.

Forsythia, precisely in the moment
Before blooming, is irrepressible
Like the sun behind thinning clouds.

In the evening, after rain,
A double rainbow, flawless
From foot to foot; the way
It arches above the house,
Seems imagined, the light
Is like an inner voice.

I am surprised again
By that moment when happiness
Is born as a return to something
Known and longed for.
The smiling nature brings out
The smiles within.

"An ever-fixed mark"*

For Alisa and Stefano

Love has altered, the house no longer feels like home,
But on this Easter Sunday, the two of you and I scan
The iambs of the sonnet, marching in the sunlit field
At the Avalon Park: there, out of the woods, in full spring
Your voices shout, "looks on tempests and is never shaken,"
Your shoes are stomping syllables on the ground.
In the rhythm you hear the beating heart of language
Return to what is comforting, tried, and known.

Dearest ones, let us remain at ease,
Unfazed, unbroken in this heartbreaking year.
Love is not love, till it meets a wall, and measures up
To loss. We concentrate, stomp on the paths, move on
Some place we can't imagine yet, our walking
The "ever-fixed mark," the rest, "brief hours and weeks."

*Shakespeare, *Sonnet 116*

Orthodox Easter, 2022

By now even the faith has got it wrong,
The Patriarch held hands with the invader
And praised the unjust war with crossed candles.

The faithful broke ranks, the filigreed eggs
Sat in baskets like stones, the sweet bread
Laid on the table like a closed book.

And us, aghast at what love means
In different homes, to different people,
Are unable to choose a place to pray,

Except God's true garden: the forests,
And the sea marshes, where
Great white herons dance in pairs

Just above our heads, their sinewy necks
Above still water: love in mirrors – free,
Wild, calling out the pink crab apple blooms.

The dwarf pines send forth long cones,
An offering of sunlit candles.
Christ rises on great heron's wings.

Whatever Happens

Whatever happens in your ravaged mind
Is not to be scoffed at, or discounted, or laughed at.

After these two years,
I feel as if I lived
A thousand mangled seasons,
Seen a thousand hurtful ages,
A thousand scorned truths,
And on our children's faces I have seen
Only very tired looks – tell-tales
Of hopelessness they must endure –
At least until we can accept the loss,
Written here, like this, in your face,
That once was their refuge.

Mother's Day, 2022

Happy Is the Heart
For Alisa and Stefano

Happy is the heart that learns
Tranquility early in life,
Keeps off the dangerous path
Where every turn brings injury.

This morning, cherry petals
Come to our windows like butterflies.
When one house burns to the ground
People build another, bolt the door
To lock the anger out.

Learn to let go of hurtful things.
Life has many kinds of hunger.
The destructive hunger is not the same
As the joyful appetite that helps you
Grow tall and strong.

We are neither saints nor angels.
Turn away from blows, do not take them.
The others' burdens are not yours to carry,
But you must carry gracefully your own.
Believe in steady hope, the miracle of love.

Stony Brook, 12 May 2022

Leaving You

I remembered today how, as a child,
I sat by old neighbors as they died.

Birds trilled in trees; the sun made spots
On the clay floor in their kitchens,

And as I held their hands, a candle
Burning at the bedside, I learned

How the journey with one another ends
Breath after breath into the forever
After.

June 8, 2022

A Hundred Eyes

I can see us with a hundred eyes –
Glimpses of moments across
Years – the best never in photographs.

Our life together, a kaleidoscope, fanciful,
Deceiving. And yet, shards of images
Tumble in a wistful pattern across countries.

*

With a hundred eyes I see death
Walking towards me with its bag of bones,
Life is remembering the before-self.

I am falling with a hundred eyes
Trained on darkness, the belly filled with
Snakes. Soon I will drink from Lethe.

*

Beyond forgetting, something new awaits.
A graceful peacock steals the sea-blue
With its feather eyes – folding and unfolding.

The sun will return in my belly,
My children's gentle laughter will set
My heart in rhythm once again.

*

Once again, I will glimpse a hundred
Dreams of what-could-have-been:
But then I will see far beyond pain.

Beyond pain I will sing a hundred songs.
With a hundred eyes I will unfold the beauty
Of this world – a new map for our children.

Stony Brook, 15 June 2022

Pictured Rocks, July 2022

For Alisa and Stefano

Hiawatha

Like the earth, our selves are built
From the battering of wind and water.
The ice and heat of feelings are ageless.
But I wouldn't know how to say

That the soul is as old as the world.
So, we drive again hundreds of miles,
Soon after the hospice doctors visit
Your grandfather in the living room.

We cross the Mackinac Bridge once more,
Follow the Lake Michigan shoreline,
Buffeted by wind and whitecaps, until
We reach deep into the Hiawatha Forest,

Where a different life awakens us.
Hawks glide just above the car; we can see
Their powerful bodies, read their wings.
Tiny lakes seem opaline, sapphire-like, cobalt-blue.

Maple birch, Northern white cedar, aspen,
Black pine, jack pine, black spruce, oak,
Elm, ash, red maple, balsam poplar, tamarack
Paper birch – and us, silent, driving North.

Here, there were shallow seas, near-shore deltas,
Sediments, sand layers, deposits of glacial drift.
In two hours, we'll see bedrock where the shoreline rises
Above the mesmerizing, cold waters of Lake Superior.

We'll read the story of hardship and time in the colors
Of the cliffs. We'll learn how those who break and die
In our family deposit sediments, build layers within us.
Healing ferns and moss will embrace and ease our grief.

Chapel Rock

Along the Hiawatha paths there is soothing music
Constantly changing. Ferns rustle, frogs hop among
Fallen leaves, chipmunks and squirrels scratch the bark,
Birds carry sweet songs from branch to branch.

Waterfalls have the sound of imagined rain
Joining the forest chorus like a memory
That visits the attuned mind. We walk until
The falls fall out of hearing, into the thinning

Line of cedars. Out on the shore, the waves
Of Lake Superior pound the Cambrian sandstone.
The water-rich breeze tickles the forest floor.
The undergrowth whispers and laughs.

We emerge next to the roof of the Chapel Rock,
Named by European sailors ages ago: it is an earth-made
House of prayer, hallowed out, with an inner room
Where the wind says a million things in this hour.

A lone white pine grows on the roof-shaped sandstone,
Strong and tall, proof of miracles, resilience in adversity:
Its living roots exposed over the precipice, drawing
Nourishment from the mainland. Roots are a bridge.

The pine is five times my age, the arch of the chapel
Collapsed three decades before I was born, leaving
The tree to stand – a guardian of rocks in the path of winds,
Alive with bird song, verdant and proud in its solitude.

House finch, pheasant, red-eyed vireo, American redstart,
Ovenbird and common raven make a music we would
Not have known unless we walked these paths.
We will return to this shore, make it a home.

The Miners' Castle

Right there, at the very edge of the golden cliff
And out of reach for us, who still walk the earth,
Perched on the rock shaped like a castle
Raised to guard the coast, a family of golden eagles.

Oh, they are so free and fearless, scanning
Water, sky, and clouds, looking down at us,
Who would shout for joy in this crazy wind
But remain transfixed, locked in their power.

Munising Falls

For Alisa and Stefano

There is a place where you can touch
The temple of the earth.
This morning's walk in the fresh, humid air,
Takes us along the woods-graced path
Along a pellucid stream, upwards
Towards the sound of the waterfalls
Merging into hearing through our footfalls.

But we linger halfway, because up the steps,
Along the path, the rock appears
Sand-golden, full of secrets,
The earth now like a wrinkled forehead.

You smile – my two joyful discoverers:
Blowholes in sandstone cliffs, sunlit water,
Backlit birch leaves. The cliff feels like
A temple deep in thought. We touch it,
Lean into it, crawl into crevices, laugh.

Time seems suspended in this peace
The same way the water seems suspended
As it falls over the precipices of the cliffs,
Always, always, always like this, we pray.

Along the Bluffs at Empire

"I feel like I am walking with my old self."
"The trees are talking, listen to the trees!"
"I am regaining strength."

And so, here we are again, meeting the old path
Where we reinforce the backbone of endurance.
The madness is behind us, at least for now.

But as we walk in this tree-swaying wind
I wonder how to put order in our lives,
How to make it so that our path remains clear.

When we arrive at the edge of the bluff
Where trees have made way for sand bushes
That carry fragrance of burnt sugar,

We see Lake Michigan at its most
Perfect steel-blue moment. Nothing like it,
You say, nothing more beautiful. A reward

Of the road, after hundreds of miles of highways
Byways, forest roads so narrow and so secret
That a hawk flew like a guide just above

The windshield, and stopped in the tree
To look at us, as we drove slowly between
The rows of cattails on each side.

Memorize the moments, keep them
As currency meant to avert the hardship
That is to come. Keep the images,

Make them last as a happy worry-free summer.
You were not given the chance
For inner peace this time.

Keep these moments in your pockets,
We will use them when it's time:
The steel-blue lake in the sand-rising wind,
The trees that talk in slow, wise voices,
The song of birds, the long dune trails.

Last Night

Last night's rain wiped off this July,
Turned the gutters into hoses,
Washed the driveway clean
Of all the sand I brought
Home from Sleeping Bear
In the car tires
And the children's shoes.

The hospice doctor will step
On the cleaned porch,
Walk into the house
That has been cursed with thunder
And lighting all night long.

July 2022

Don't Speak of Time
For my father

I asked the doctor not to speak of time:
Not of weeks, months, not
Of filling the prescriptions every two weeks,
No one knows when it's time, I said,
Let him not know if it's this week or that.

I said this in English but I know
My father listened in Romanian,
Too clever to pay attention to words,
When my voice and the doctor's met
In the thick air across the table.

At home he asked, what are you worrying about,
I die a happy man: you didn't end up
Living in *that* country, I paid your school debt,
You've done with your life as you wanted,
And I lived long enough to give your son my shirts.
It's my time to go, I must make place for others.

His argument was crisp and clear.
We stood and said goodbye,
He shook hands with my son,
Kissed my daughter, said to her
"We'll dance at Christmas," then
Looked at me with resolute eyes
That somehow still worried
More than the command, "Be strong."
What remains of our time together
Is glimpsed between our voices and our words.

It's Possible

Time flows backwards,
Receding river,
Narrowing,
Returning to its spring
Like a secret.
Or a broken egg
Yearning for its shell.

I read the signposts
In the mother tongue,
Which I imagine
I have forgotten.
Before knowing, the soul
Gathers upon itself,
Grows the past
Around it.

Like an egg, the soul
Is ready to break again.
Like a river, the soul is ready
To rush over the banks.

Watkins Glen, Finger Lakes

Stone-made steps,
Water stepping off stones
Water falling over the stones,
Eternal veil
Never to be lifted
Off the face
Of this cliff.

I walk behind the veil
Reach into falling water.
I look, and I see
What the falling water sees:
The winding path
Of the canyon,
Small water pools
Filled with sunlight,
Or reflections of trees.
Glistening steps
That lead to a bridge
Filled with people,
Crossing.

The Erratic Heart

For my mother

How lucky we all were that I was there
When you tapped lightly on my shoulder
In the dead of night. "My heart is beating
Too fast, and then too slow. We need
The doctors, I think." You still talk about that.

Before we knew it, I found my way
On the seat next to the ambulance driver
Who leaned towards me the whole way
Explaining that we will reach the hospital
On time, and the paramedics in the back
Are doing very well at keeping you stable.

The monitors, the tests, the IV bags,
And now the phone calls: the episodes
Keep returning since I left.
There must be a pacemaker to make peace
In your failing heart. It isn't a failing heart.

*

I am 800 miles away in a surgery room,
Fighting with things that grow inside of *me*
Out of the natural order. The utensils
On the table, the lights, the nurse
Whose soft hands wrap around my right hand,
The doctor who sedates me
Before he makes me sleep.
You know I will call once they wake me up.

A Wedding Dream

For Cătălin

Life has a way to right all wrongs,
For there, in the picture you just sent
From Lake Michigan, there is a ring
On the hand of the one you love,
The champagne flute filled –
And of course, greenery and sun.

As if God means to say:
Trust that ahead the path is filled
With surprises you'd be glad for:
New lives, new hopes, other reasons
To get up in the mornings:
The thrills of love, promises.

So here we are mixing languages
Like drinks: two-three, one-two,
All for the youngest in the family,
The one who now must take his seat
At the marriage table, taste the gifts.

September 2022

Twenty-Five Monarch Butterfly Crossings

For Stefano

They were dancing across the walking path
Between inlet and open sea. But how did you
Think of counting each time they came around?

These days pass as surprisingly as each
Monarch butterfly crossing our path.
I count days the way you count butterflies.

September 19, 2022

Your Time

For my father

I am swaddled in white
A white bow on top of a baby hat.
I gaze straight into your eyes
Yawning at the beginning of my life.

In the picture, you sit holding me
In your arms, your hands
Securely fastened around
My shoulders and my feet;

You look as if you are
Stooping from the weight
Of tenderness as you
Smile at me, your first-born.

And you are wearing a black suit
A white shirt, a tie, your hair
Thick with dark curls: it's one
Year after your release from prison.

*

Of course, I want to turn
Back the time to the moment
When I fit in the crook of your arm
And I am entirely gift.

I do not see marks from chains
On your wrists in that picture.
I see the two of us, seated
Formally for the image of our lives,
Not knowing you are a hero.

*

I am speaking with you from
West Meadow Beach, around
The time the sun sets: the golden glow
Over the water feels like your words.

Your speech is slurred
But your mind rings
Clear as a bell, and you sing to me
That song, "I wait for you to return."
I ask you to wait for me
Because in my heart I am not well,
I am not ready. And I know you
Will wait, as you did before.

*

I am on the plane imagining
Myself a white crane,
In my mind I fly East,
The plane is flying North-West.

What happens to our faces
Because of time, you mused once
Looking at me after years
Of distance. Time distends the skin,

Shrivels it, writes on our faces
The story of the roads.
Look. Out of the plane I will emerge
As a tiny boat out of the mother ship.

We are turning in the air,
We will land soon. Soon I will hold
Your hands in mine. It's not time
Yet for your crossing.

*

"I remember when you were smaller
Than a goose," you say. "I remember
The watermelon farm, you and your sister
Swimming in the Caras River."

So many memories flood your
Hours in the night, you say.
"You always slept on my chest,
And you never let me rest."

"What happened to the Grizzly, Daddy?"
I remember the safety of your chest.
Mom makes a Moldavian meal:
Your youngest pours you a glass of wine.

"I am dancing with the old age," you say.
We drink together knowing
What we know. But there is no grief.
You sit among us tonight.

Holy Communion

For my parents

The priest gathered us under the cross
In our living room, parents seated,
Children kneeling. The book opened,
The words of old prayers flew about
Like freed doves, trained to return home.

*

We don't know if my brother opened
The last bottle of wine, or if I protested
Dad's dying one last time, when I offered
The glass of red instead of the morphine,
Because, for God's sake, we'll do this right.

Mom and my sister nursed dad through
The small hours, talking softly about
What will happen to all of us scattered
Too far from home. Dad told us to plant
A row of fruit trees, fix the writers' shed.

*

It's Sunday morning. The sun rises
In the autumn-burned trees, above our church.
The priest alone waits for us with holy oil,
Holy wine, incense, prayers, and songs.
My brother, my sister and I walk through

The door. We light three candles. Our faces
Are reflected in the face of Christ glowing
In the icon lit by stained-glass-windows-sunrise.

The priest calls us to the altar, where we
Drink the tiny spoon of wine. Peace.

*

I walk alone to the room I filled with flowers
Nearly seventeen years ago, preparing
For my wedding. The mind has a way
Of layering parts of our lives, so that dying
Father, lost marriage, and those August roses

Reflect each other in the memory of icons
I kiss this morning. My father's cold hands
Are in mine: "Bravo," he says
When I kiss him all over his face, "Bravo."
"I'll stay a little longer," he says, "You fly home."

Grand River is covered in glowing fog
In the growing morning. Maples emerge
Candle-like orange through dewy ribbons
Above the water. And I take flight
Through the thick cloud, up towards the sun.

Sunday, 16 October 2022

Solstitium

For Pramila

It wasn't just a feeling:
The sun stood still,
The light in the hours was weak
And the ravens came out,
Curious about us being there.
They were black like ink.
Perched on the high branches,
They surveilled us.

As if from the longest night
The ravens came out on top of trees
And looked us in the eye.
You turned away from them
Sensing how I was drawn
By their powerful wings
That beat above us.

The sun stood still,
The light in the hours was weak,
So much like this time of my life,
When luck stands still.
The ravens were feasting in the fields
I loved their powerful beaks
They took my soul under their wings,
It wasn't just a feeling.

We counted the ravens – two
And then three, five, more –
They flew so low in the fields
As I walked after them.
I walked with the ravens in the fields.

*

I had forgotten that it was the shortest day,
When I asked you to join me.
All I wanted was a walk in the fields,
We always see hawks and herons there,
We look for omens about going away
From here. My luck stands still.

The ravens did not speak to me
From the tops of trees. They looked
At us as fellow travelers and left.
The water in the sea was clear.
I've come through the longest night,
You see, my dear. The Earth continues
To tilt: it's not just a feeling.

December 21–22, 2022

Memento Mori
For my father

The mortician gave you a smile you never had
Your folded hands upon the cross felt like wax
The grandchildren kept exchanging the tiny icons
We placed upon on your chest, nothing felt right.

*

I'd like to believe that in the first morning
When your soul left your old, tired body
You sent the gift of secret strength
To all of us, according to our want and need.

*

To whom do I owe these glorious mornings,
When the sun makes the sky manifest as a soul?
I owe these mornings of hope to the kind
And merciful God, who made you and made me.

Inside the grave of yellow clayish soil
At the Vatra Monastery in Michigan
Your body does its own journey of returning
To the dust of this earth. It's peaceful there.

*

In the end you agreed with me about us
Becoming nothing but stories, sharing
No more than memories half-remembered
When the body grows tired of itself.

"Hai, stati sa ne mai amintim" *Come, stay a bit,*
Let us remember for a little while. But this morning
My words feel as rigid as the sick and dying body,
Weak in recalling the last moments when we spoke.

My poem fails to give you the presence you had.
Your folded words upon the final prayers feel like wax.
The grandchildren keep listening to your final voicemails
That sing you alive in our ears. Nothing feels right.

29 December 2022

Ray of Sunlight

Over there, by the sea,
        Sunrays turn into ladders
                Unfolding through the clouds.
                    Today, I want to drink
                            This half-empty cup of sky
                    And climb the sunray ladders,
            Until, blinded by light,
        I never look back at the ground.

                    *

The sound of happy laughter
Tumbling down the stairs
In our once happy house.
Sunshine in winter-reflecting mirrors.
Over there, in memory,
How beautiful the ground…

Stony Brook, January 12–13, 2023

Archer Street

Today I met an old man who was lost,
He stood between
Yorkshire and Archer, I don't know
Where I am, he said,
I don't know how to go home,
I think it's number 44, he said,
But I can't remember the street name.

It was freezing cold out there,
I was about to turn around
But the old man stood lost
And his eyes had that look
That is unforgettable – that pulls –
I don't know where I am, he said.

Don't worry, everyone forgets, I said,
I will help you find your way home,
Let's look at the numbers on the mailboxes
To see if we can find 44 on these streets
But the numbers were small: 4, 5, 6
We kept turning around in the cold.

Don't worry, I said, I will help you
Find the way home. I am here visiting
My daughter, he said, she is a doctor.
Do you have her phone number, I asked.
We called her and found the address –
It was a pleasant walk
Once we knew where we were going.

We talked about his countries, Afghanistan, Pakistan,
And mine, Romania, and how parents dream big
For their children after wars end, or after

Families get away. His eyes were warm and calm
But he kept forgetting names and dates
The way one slips on an oily kitchen floor
And I kept saying "fine" as if everything made sense.

But then again, everything *makes* sense:
He is an old father in a new country visiting his daughter,
Memory is fragile like a porcelain cup in a child's hands,
Elusive like the foam of the sea when you catch it in your palm,
It runs away from you like a gap in breathing
When you are in the middle of a street you've never seen before,
It tricks you into believing strangers are your family.
You are my sister, he said, thank you for bringing me home.

I never know how streets are named
But I wonder about the precision of archery,
The target and the aim of mind, eye, arm,
The hands that hold the bow and arrow,
The trajectory of memory.
I wonder if and how
The gap in remembering his younger
Daughter's name, her husband's exact
Specialty in medicine, whether home now
Is Afghanistan abandoned during a war
Or Pakistan where his girls went to university
And this freezing street, where we met
Have something to do with how we lose thoughts
And bits of ourselves along the way,
And find company
And gratitude even when
The road behind us disappears
Leaving us waiting, confused
Away from home.

Sixteen

For Stefano

You've grown so tall, you tower over me,
Just like I dreamed you would.
We talk about life the way I imagine
The ancient thinkers talked when they walked:
About why people are the way we see them,
Why they do things that surprise us.

But on this day, the heart is stricken,
And words fail me in ways they never did before.
Away with suffering, I say, away!
I'd give the world for your face filled with smiles,
For your laughter filling up the house,
For your trust that everything ahead is bright.

Your Soul Is Nowhere to Be Found

There is darkness everywhere, traps abound
We're searching for your soul, but our feet are bound
Darkness grows on darkness, all around.

You're jumping on a trampoline in the living room
The anger inside you thumps inside this doom
We wonder whose emptiness is for whom.

We're searching for your soul, but our feet are bound
The anger inside you thumps the sound of gloom
Darkness grown on darkness, all around.

Bird Lament

Across the world there is signal of a nest:
It looks like a mirage above the desert sands
That sing with stories of four thousand years.

Here in the verdant garden turned to weeds
They have clipped my wings, past the middle
Of my life, after I have earned the right to fly.

March 15, 2023

Sea, Wind, Moon

I wonder what you feel when you glimpse
The moon above our house, in the bare trees.

This March the birdsong rises early
In the mornings. I rise

Early with the bird song, dreaming
To pack a backpack and walk out

Of this house forever, to meet
The world as if for the first time.

*

I did not bury the ring as I said:
In the end, a burial is meant for those we love.

I threw it in the turbulent sea the same way
People topple statues of dictators.

The sea received our wedding ring,
Took it in its mysterious hands,

Tossed it with its water fingers:
Our marriage is no more.

West Meadow Beach, 8 March 2023

Easter 2023

for Alisa and Stefano

The Christian spirit rises on great wings,
The church at the corner is overfilled,
But the mother is banished from home:
She'd raised her children, has aged, is unemployed.

Alone, the children take to the street. In less than the time
It takes for the Holy Week to pass, they learn
To catch venomous snakes without getting hurt,
They can hold turtles in the cups of their hands.

The son paddles the sea and helps clean the village island:
He keeps for his mother a gift of deer teeth.
The daughter fills the house with wildflowers.
Ospreys circle overhead. Their banished mother returns.

April 9, 2023

Since You Died, the Earth Turned Green

For my father

It's May again, the grave is green and healed,
The cemetery trees are filled with birdsong,
And my son shows me the cormorants
Above the Mill Pond, carrying
Branches in their beaks to their island nests.

Mom, Loredana, and the priest sang
On your birthday. They poured wine
On your grave and around the cross,
And now I wonder if it's peaceful
Where you are, if you hear the noise of time.

You loved birds. Today my son took me
And his sister to his secret place, where
Great Herons have set up their nests: they look
Like white candles in the trees. Candles
With wings: like us driving home in the night
This year, with lit Easter candles in our hands.

Enheduana

You come to me in the abyss of marriage
"Yours is the oven that is full of food, of basketfuls of bread,"
And call me to the ancient Sumer, where you say,
"Your roots toil with heaven and earth:" *

True, over thousands of years on, and truer still
Because the land itself calls me home
From across the world. I will travel South
To the Tropic of Cancer, then East across the ocean.

*

Here the earth is verdant, blossoming into Spring,
There the world bakes in the sand. Tell me, Enheduana,
What to do with my words this Holy Week
When my soul toils with heaven and earth.

He spat on my oven full of food,
Walked over my baskets full of bread,
Soiled the marriage bed, left the children crying,
And my heart toiling with heaven and earth.

*

I will go South, Enheduana, and fly East.
There, in eternal sunshine, the egrets will play
Tricks of memory on me, toiling with heaven and earth,
But my oven shall be full of food, baskets filled with bread.

My children will play in the mangroves,
They will leave their suffering behind, Enheduana.

Teach me the healing words from woman to woman,
Teach my words to rejoice in heaven and earth.

* 'The Temple Hymns' from *The Complete Poems of Enheduana: the world's first author*, trans. Sophus Helle, p. 57-8

Wedding in Riga

The time has come to say the sacred marriage words,
You, dearest brother, a hearty veteran in new homelands,
Your bride, beautiful and bright as the light of June.

Today we celebrate with Honor Guard and Sword Arch in Church,
Home is where love is, and love is a house with many rooms,
Each room, a secret between the two of you.

Two languages have joined to offer sacred marriage words,
You, dearest brother, a hearty veteran in new homelands.

I remember you as a little child filled with joy,
Today we bring our love for your new, tender world.
May your marriage thrive, strengthen its roots, and grow.

In our family you are the youngest who brings joy.
Today our father is at the wedding feast in spirit,
He'd have been proud to see you take your vows.
Mother is at your side, you give her so much joy,
Today we bring our love for your new, tender world.

For Cătălin and Eliza, Riga, 10 June 2023

White Sand

I arrived in a white storm.
The land is cut up and parceled:
Bulldozers, workers, cranes.

Wind blows over the sand.
Palms sway in the wind.
The sun scorches the whiteness.

It is not possible to breathe outside.
The white haze shrouds the roads,
Bridges, islands, and the city.

At night the red moon hovers
Over the hives of bulldozers,
Cranes, workers, and dust.

*

The sand looks like snow.
The city appears and vanishes
In the white clouds.

White sand dervishes swirl
Beyond the windows.
In the morning, haze stifles sun.

The wind blows again
And this time the city appears
Glittering and glimmering.

In this land without rain,
I have memorized the smell
Of hot burning sand,

Learned the panic of heat rising
From beneath my feet; wrapped
Myself in the hot milky gauze

Of the white sandstorm.
These days it feels as if
The sky fell upside-down.

*

Since I have gone, my children
Speak their love to me
In a new language: they prepare

The meals we used to make,
They use the recipes I learned
As a child from my mother.

In the freshly baked loaves
They have kneaded all that I am
To them. White sand, I pray you

Swallow my bitter heart
And give me a heart of light
For my journey back home,

Keep the pain of life I brought
To you. White hot sand,
You called me, and I came.

Abu Dhabi August 4-12, 2023

Twelve

For Alisa

The boxes are opened and unpacked,
You and your brother assembled the bookshelves.
Here in our new, light-filled house,
You twirl, all smiles, your hair a golden waterfall
Behind you. You are ready for your friends,
Your favorite cake, and the gifts I brought
From far away – too far to mention.

Oh, dear one, you have grown so much
These twelve summers, now you have
Reached my height and look into my eyes.
Woods across the road at the front door,
More woods at the back the house,
A spacious porch that we will fill with flowers:
We will heal here, before we go on.

Porcelain Cups

For my mother

Our set of espresso cups
With light-pink roses
Painted in a garden setting
Contained by borders of gold,
Has travelled softly and unharmed
Across the ocean, and from there
In suitcases and in boxes again.

But these days, I am so tense,
Everything I hold in my hands
Cracks: there is only one
Crystal champagne flute left.

I saved the fissured coffee cups,
(With their dead-end porcelain
Paths through torn rose gardens)
Into nests of tissue paper.
I placed them in the cupboard
Until my hands learn not
To hold the dearest things too tight.

7 October 2023

West River Drive

For my mother

The priest painted Dad's room on Sunday,
One month and two days after he died,
And he became an imagined presence.

In my mind's eye I bend towards his pillow
To kiss his forehead, I try to hold his gaze,
But memory is a misleading path.

You threw away his bed, the curtains;
I took his black suit in his carryon suitcase;
Loredana drove all his tools to her house.

Dad's garage is dismantled,
Our pictures are in boxes,
And you prepare to sell the house.

What will happen to your dahlias,
The gladioli and the tiger lilies,
That feeling of coming home to find you?

Two days ago, a bald eagle danced above
My rented house. Grief finds us
In one place and takes us to another.

I want to know where you are going,
Because I want to come with you,
Let us travel together for a while.

East Setauket, 30 September–7 October 2023

"From the beginning of time until now."
For M

Article 1:
As I understand, the phrase exists in litigation
To stop us from going back in time, to claim whatever
We might think was wrongfully withheld.

Article 2:
But this morning I see things differently:
Who can ever imagine the beginning of time,
Even between two people who just met

Article 3:
And set the clock in motion for their
Hopes together? "Now" is the relevant
Word, because the clock has stopped

Article 4:
Where we are: in a room with documents
Where the only other words that matter
In the dissolution of the union are

Article 5:
"Affirmatively asserts." Well, I assert
I own no worldly things, though I'll
Do so not "affirmatively." Let us talk

Article 6:
About heavenly possessions then:
Hopes, feelings, dreams? From the time
I can remember, I swear, I never lost them.

7 October 2023

Travels

Riga,
    Dublin,
        Abu Dhabi,
            London,
                Oxford,
                    Cambridge,
                        Lindisfarne
And back again to court and lawyers' offices and injured souls,
The three of us packing and unpacking, litigating each visa stamp
On our passports, leaving scans of our eyes across the world.

Jubail mangroves
Seals' chorus in the North Sea
Oscar Wilde's statue in a Dublin park
The Canal, the Backs, the punts
Homes filled with smiling friends

Then back again to court and lawyers' offices and injured souls,
The three of us packing and unpacking, litigating each visa stamp
On our passports, leaving scans of our eyes across the world.

Hawk

I went out to look at him –
An apparition with great wings
Glowing in the light of morning,
Scanning below the spring tree line.
I returned inside and drank my tea
Without losing sight of him.
The orioles put on alarm calls,
Mockingbirds attacked him,
He now cleans his feathers, unperturbed,
At the very top of the tallest tree.

I think about my deadlines
And the morning sliding by,
But he watches my garden
From way up there.
I am hooked on him
Against the flawless sky
With flowering trees below,
Time pulls the two of us along,
In the bright, fresh morning.

Under him, such a tiny tree branch
Sustains unbearable weight,
Fragility seems only an illusion.
Hawk, take everything that is weak in me
In your claws: eat it.
Leave me wise and patient.
It's been nearly two hours since
You appeared, and straightened me
From the spine up, eyes on you.

April 8, 2024

Solar Eclipse

Snowy egrets flew low,
Waded at the water's edge.

A blue-grey heron
Roosted on the yellow magnolia.

Cormorants flapped their wings
On the floating trunks in the pond.

Geese talked in pairs.
Swans napped over their nests.

A row of turtles sunned themselves.
The moon slid over the sun like an eyelid

And everything went cool and quiet.
My kids whispered of sunset,

The spring flowers glowed in the odd light.
And then the moon slid off the sun

Returning all the songs to the birds.
We are changed forever, having seen

The night inside the day, having
Felt the flight of snowy herons.

April 8, 2024

Farewell West Meadow

for Pramila

Low flying Great Herons,
Lighting-bright things.

Swans take off the pond:
Clamorous, water-beating wings.

Ospreys claw their fish,
Stand guard at the trailhead.

You, who walk with me
Help me see ahead.

Birthday at Sleeping Bear
For Alisa

What joy this is, a full fresh cherry pie
And people singing Happy Birthday
In the morning by the lake!

You bring this August to a close
Over a day climbing the back
Of Momma Bear, barefoot.

And you dance in azure waters
Thirteen times making my heart sing.
At night you and your brother

Lead me back to the dunes.
We walk among stargazers
And run, arms outstretched,

Over the Sleeping Bear, while
She rests covered in the blanket
Of the Milky Way, her paws in water.

30 August 2024
Sleeping Bear Dunes National Lakeshore

The Toy House

The wind swoops over the fields,
Like a ravenous turkey vulture.

My mother bandages her wounded leg
And walks away from death every day:

She counts the miles, makes her report
When she steps back into her house.

*

It's useless to wish a house of stone
For newlyweds: here the walls

Are made of plastic and tin,
The homes are brought to the fields

On wheels, they are set
On tiny bricks: ambitions on stilts.

*

In the day, the sound of tires
Lines the motorway like a ribbon,

The trucks' engines protest
So much night transport,

Only now and then I can hear
Geese and cranes calling.

*

The skin continues to learn
Of solitudes year after year,

Chastity after betrayal is reassuring
As a cocoon, or lover's touch

Before the wedding vows.
The nights run wild with the coyotes

Among the plastic and tin houses
In these marshes, vast fields.

I find the mornings at the kitchen
Windows and cling to them

As a child cries and grabs
The mother's skirt, following her.

9 September 2024

Sandhill Cranes

Two sandhill cranes walk across
The school sidewalk,
Before the morning bell:

Out of place and yet unstartled,
Like my daughter and my son
Going to a new school.

*

We have traveled across the map
But I discover there is still
A long journey ahead,

With feelings that cling,
And call us back,
Keeping us awake at night:

Almost a month now waiting
For our clothes and books,
The coffee mug, the pans

All wrapped in boxes,
The truck that soon will
Bring battered memories to us.

Chelsea, Michigan, September 9, 2024